Cordelia Ryan Twomey, Ph.D.

REBRAND YOURSELF
FOR
TOMORROW'S WORKFORCE

ISBN: 978-1-7366897-1-4 (Paperback)
ISBN: 978-1-7366897-0-7 (eBook)

Cover design by Berge Design

To my three guardian angels, who kept me on track—

Maria, Marian, and Richard.

I could not have done it without you.

Contents

Introduction

In recent times, the job market has changed, and people from all walks of life are entering and reentering the job market. Competition is fierce, and repackaging yourself must be your first priority.

You are marketing a product—you—and it is the packaging of the product that is so important.

Is the job landscape the same as a year ago? Six months ago? No. The job market has definitely been reconfigured and our goal is to prepare you to enter that new job market.

Why did I write this book? All of us have at least one thing that we do well, and for me it's helping people get jobs and promotions by organizing their experiences in a way that is logical and easy for the reader to follow. I have taught college students throughout my career, and helping my students get jobs has always been a priority. I have also helped many friends at the university organize their work so that they can get promotions. An expression I frequently use is "It ain't brain surgery." Just follow the rules. Give the reader what they want. This is not an exercise in creative writing. Just report the facts in an interesting, easy-to-understand way.

I have written this book as if we were sitting and having coffee. The tone is conversational. I am going to say "we" a lot because we are in this together. Your success means that I have done my job.

How does this book apply directly to you? It is designed to serve as an information cornerstone as well as a source of motivation—information by providing resources, and motivation to get you doing the things that you should be doing if you are serious about the job hunt. The book is written from a perspective of tough love. My job is to push you, prod you, and encourage you to your goal. I know that there are millions of websites and books on the topic of finding a job. This book provides a simple, practical approach to this project by breaking the job hunt down into small, manageable steps. Most importantly, it is customizable because you include those components that are most appropriate to *your* job hunt.

Who are the people to whom this book is targeted?

- Workers who thought their jobs were secure and who have suddenly become unemployed
- Consultants and gig workers who worked job to job— and now the industries that hired them have changed or disappeared
- Retirees who have found their fixed incomes negatively impacted and who have to re-enter the job market
- People who have had changes in their domestic circumstances such as divorce or illness or death of a partner
- First-time job seekers graduating from high school or college
- People who currently have a job and who seek to advance in their careers

Here is how to use this book:

The people reading this book will come from many different walks of life, each with its own unique requirements. Yet there are many elements that the job hunt has in common.

There are three main focal points:

- Chapter 1, Planning for the Job, provides a baseline of information and skill sets for all readers. Here we pull together our resources, conduct our job-hunt research, and begin our job-hunt campaign.

- If I had to say which part is most important, hands down it is chapter 1. Planning is not the part of the process that most people find exciting. Jumping in and doing it are much more fun. However, you can't "jump in" if you don't know where to jump or what you're jumping into. What we want to design is a marketing plan that is clear, positive, and error free. Yes, you are designing a marketing plan because you are marketing a product— you. If your plan is well designed, the execution will be simple and will go just as you envisioned it.
- Chapter 2, Getting the Job, is where we execute the plan. This chapter provides a detailed walk-through from getting into the right mind-set for the interview to the interview itself to the follow-up plan.
- Chapter 3, It's Never Too Early: The Portfolio, is the chapter where we discuss the importance of a portfolio during many stages of your work life—getting a job, keeping a job, and moving up in the organization.

Another feature of this book are the checklists found at the end of almost every section. The list is designed to reinforce what we just talked about in the previous section as well as to kick-start your actions. At the end of each checklist, space has been left for you to enter additional information. As we go through the sections, go back through the checklists and be honest with yourself—did you do the previous tasks on the list?

Chapter 1

Planning for the Job

This is a marketing campaign and you are marketing a product—*you*! Don't think that you can't do it. You can! You can because we are going to attack this project in what I refer to as "chunklets"—small, manageable pieces.

Section 1. Survey the Landscape

Someone once gave me a great piece of advice:

People who were in the canal boat business and saw themselves in the canal boat business were destined for failure.

People who were in the canal boat business and saw themselves in the transportation business were destined for success.

Take a long, hard look at the industry you are familiar with. Where is that industry headed? In a positive direction or toward extinction? There is an expression that has been around for years and which fits here: "Skate to where the puck is going, not where it has been."

Be aware of a phrase called "creative destruction." In its simplest form, it means that a new industry has emerged that causes another to dry up. A clear example is Amazon's impact on the brick-and-mortar retail industry. Is your field still relevant? If not, how can you reinvent yourself, playing on your strengths such as analysis, management, communication, design, and many more that you may have used in your previous jobs?

Survey the landscape. Is your area of expertise accounting? Engineering? Communication? Marketing? What does the future hold for that industry? If it is not promising, let's find a field to which you can transfer your skills and abilities. Let's get going. Three key words are important to keep in mind: *procedures*, *technology*, and *people*.

Procedures

The procedures are the rules that you set for yourself—the routines, the timelines, and the discipline that help you to complete this challenge. They can include naming policies for your files, starting work at a certain time each day, getting up for lunch in another area outside your "office," and going for a walk each day.

- Create a workspace. Don't work in bed. Create a mind-set. Don't work in your pajamas. Get dressed. This is a job...this is your current job.
- Create a work schedule. Set aside a strict block of hours each day to work on this job.
- Identify your work habits. Realize what your time wasters are and work on reducing or ignoring them.
- Set realistic, concrete timelines. When do you envision having a job? Don't say "as soon as possible." That's too vague. Use backward planning. Say, "I want to have a job by [three months from now]." If so, when do you need to start sending out your cover letters and résumés? When do you see the interviews starting?
- Create and maintain a calendar for accountability where you can put your finger on any date and know exactly where you should be at that point. If you cannot envision the end result, how can anyone else?
- Your job search should be your priority. Learn to say "no" when friends and family ask you to do things. Save the outings for when you have a job.

- Work smart, not hard. At the end of each day you should be able to look back and quantify what you did that day—"I answered five more ads today than yesterday"; "I made six follow-up calls today"; "I set up two interviews."
- Keep your mind and body active. This will keep your creative juices flowing and your enthusiasm level high. Exercise every day. You don't need a costly gym. There are so many free online classes. Start with YouTube and see what you like. Or just go out and take a walk—do something every day.

Technology

The technology includes all the resources you need to get the job done—the physical space, the computer, the software and apps, storage devices, and yes, there is a place in this world for pen and paper.

- Create a fixed place where you will work. Whether you live in a small apartment or a ten-room house, organize your "office". Technology definitely includes the ergonomics that go into helping you work efficiently and effectively.
- Keep your resources in one place. If you are using a kitchen table that has to be repurposed each day when you have to move, put all your paperwork in a large box, rather than having materials scattered all around.
- Check your computer's audio and video capabilities.
- Check your computer's audio and video capabilities. If you don't have a camera, buy one. Also, you can use your phone as a microphone. You will see how much you will need these later.

- Make sure that you have enough supplies—paper, a flash drive, toner or ink jet cartridges...
- Buy a box of good stationery, not the usual copy grade. It is also advised that you buy a color like off-white or beige (not pink or blue) to make your résumé stand out from the crowd. You will bring hard copies of important documents with you to the interview, so make them look professional.
- Make sure that you have good lighting. Working as if you were at the bottom of a coal mine is discouraging to long-term input.
- Create a separate, new digital folder for each job you apply for. Eventually, the folder should include the job posting, the cover letter and the résumé that you submitted for that particular job, the dates and times of your interviews, the interviewers' business cards, your thank-you letter, and other items that you find helpful to you. Each folder should be a complete collection for that particular job.
- Scan all your documents. If you do not own a scanner, no need to go out and buy one. There are free scanning apps that you can put on your phone and scan the documents as if they were photographs. Then upload the documents from your phone to your website.
- Get in the habit of backing up all of your work. Your hard drive is just a machine that could crash; then everything you have worked so hard on would be lost.
- Get technological. Next year you're going to be a year older anyway, so keep thinking of ways to use technology to make your life easier.

People

The people aspect is the third key ingredient. Have you kept in touch with people from your past work, volunteer, academic, and social lives? Do you have mentors who can help?

- Create a contact list. Start letting people know that you are looking for a job. Who are "people"? Former supervisors and co-workers, friends, family members, neighbors—cast a wide net.
- Go through your phone contacts and your holiday card list. Who can help?
- Visit the websites of your previous employers. Whom could you contact?
- If you are a recent graduate, did you have a favorite teacher?
- Use LinkedIn as a way to renew old acquaintances.
- Start now to get all contact information accurate. This will sharpen your skills when you meet people during your job search. You have to get spelling and the titles correct.

You never know where a valuable contact could turn up. What is the worst thing that could happen? They say "no"? You'll never know if you don't try.

Get organized! Time is of the essence. Let's read checklist #1 and get started.

Checklist #1

Procedures, technology, and people

		Status?	Notes to self
1	Create a workspace.		
2	Post a daily work schedule and the current to do list near your computer.		
3	Realize what your time wasters are and work on reducing or ignoring them.		
4	Set timelines and keep a detailed calendar.		
5	Keep mind and body active.		
6	Check computer's audio and video.		
7	Check your supplies—paper, a flash drive, toner or ink jet cartridges, stationery, stamps.		
8	In particular, buy a box of good stationery.		
9	Make sure that you have good light.		
10	Create a separate, new digital folder for each interview and name your files clearly.		
11	Scan all your documents.		
12	Get in the habit of backing up your work frequently.		

13	Start making a contact list of people to whom you can turn for help in your job search.		
14	Use electronic resources such as LinkedIn, school faculty directories and websites to find contacts.		
15	At the end of each day, stop and assess your progress.		
16	Have your timelines been realistic?		
17	Are you maintaining your calendar of accountability?		
18			
19			
20			

Section 2. Where Do You Want to Be?

Examine where your field is today. If you want to change, what field do you want to work in? At what level can you re-enter the market or at what level are you willing to re-enter the market? It is time to reinvent yourself, to modernize for the new job market. This can be a fresh start.

In this section we want to work on the following three areas:

✓ Looking for a job
✓ Finding job titles that are similar to what you have done
✓ Updating your knowledge, skills, and language

Remember, the websites listed below are not the *only* ones for each of the topics. There are many, many more. This is just to give us a starting point. *Occupational Outlook Handbook*, TED Talks, Khan Academy MOOCs—if you ask, "What are these?," you need them more than you know. Are these the only resources you will need? No, but the material below is a great place to start.

Job Sites

There are many websites that will provide you with information about places to look for a job. Right now we are in no way ready to start the job hunt. To do so now would be extremely premature. However, I wanted you to see one example, "The 10 Best Job Search Websites of 2021" (https://www.thebalancecareers.com/top-best-job-web-sites-2064080). There are many that will say "the ten best..." or "the most successful..." Judge for yourself. Bookmark and inventory the websites that *you* find helpful for *your* job search.

Similar Jobs

Has your field morphed into something different? Find out the latest job descriptions and salary ranges through the Bureau of Labor Statistics' *Occupational Outlook Handbook* (https://www.bls.gov/ooh/). This is a valuable resource to learn about the skill sets and job descriptions related to a particular field and for you to see where your strengths could be applied.

Have you kept up with innovations in your field? Perhaps you were in the same job for many years and felt comfortable. Or you find that you are ready for a change. The *Occupational Outlook Handbook* is an excellent resource for up-to-the-minute, detailed job requirements.

Updating Knowledge, Skills, and Language

Looking for job might not be the best time to spend a lot of money on courses and tuition. There are many online resources that will bring you up to speed. Two that are highly regarded are TED Talks (https://www.ted.com/) and Khan Academy (https://www.khanacademy.org/). Find others that may be specifically related to your field.

Overheads and Slides

Just as an accountant or a teacher looking for a job today would not start talking about overheads and slides, the same is true for you. You have to use today's language. One way is to go to online presentations and classes in your field. TED Talks has a wide array of topics, with presentations led by experts in the field. In addition, Khan Academy has a section entitled "College / Adult Learner," where they have free courses for everyone from community college to graduate school students as well as adult learners.

An excellent way to take Ivy League courses and possibly get a certificate in a chosen field is to take a MOOC (massive open online course). For example, EdX (https://www.edx.org) is a non-profit created by founding partners Harvard and MIT that brings the best of higher education to students around the world. EdX offers MOOCs and interactive online classes in subjects including law, history, science, engineering, business, social sciences, computer science, public health, and artificial intelligence. The mission of EdX is to "give a world-class education to everyone, everywhere, regardless of gender, income, or social status." Let's say that you have heard a lot about blockchain in your field but did not really know what it is. You could take Blockchain Fundamentals from Berkeley

University through EdX and receive a professional certificate at the end. There may be a reasonable fee attached to courses that offer a certificate, but it could be well worth it.

If you are a college graduate, check whether your school allows you to audit courses. Many local community colleges offer reduced tuition if you are resident of that community. Also, if you are a senior citizen, see if your local community or four-year college offers discounted tuition for seniors.

Are you starting to get a feel for where do you want to be? In the next section we will see that there are common factors in all people's job hunts.

Checklist #2

Where do you want to be?

		Status?	Notes to self
1	Bookmark and inventory the websites that you have visited for your job search. Make a note of the helpfulness of each.		
2	As you bookmark sites, give them your own specific name, so you can go back and find them quickly.		
3	Did the *Occupational Outlook Handbook* help you locate descriptions of any jobs you are interested in?		
4	Did you visit the TED Talks site?		
5	Did you visit the Khan Academy site?		
6	Did you visit at least one MOOC site?		
7	Did you visit the websites of local colleges for courses that could help you?		
8	Have your timelines been realistic?		
9	Are you maintaining your calendar of accountability?		
10			

11			
12			

Section 3. A Practice Video Interview

Before you participate in your first practice video interview, inventory your strengths and acknowledge those areas you have to work on so that you will be ready for the "real" interview. The "you" today is far different from the "you" of five or ten years ago. Therefore, you should do an inventory of your strengths matched to today's requirements for any jobs you are interested in. That is where the *Occupational Outlook Handbook* is so valuable.

- Assess your skill sets. What value-added benefits do you bring to that particular position?
- Make a list of what you did well in previous positions that you can transfer to the next job. It is helpful to see these things in writing.

Make a list of areas you need to work on. See it in writing. What can you do to turn negatives into positives?

- Based on the information that you found in the *Occupational Outlook Handbook*, highlight areas where you need to brush up and expand your skill sets. As you saw previously, there is no need to spend a lot of money. Avail yourself of free online resources.

Every state and many local communities are conducting online job fairs. Use the free resources available on the internet and in your community to find them.

When I was researching material for this book I came across a New Jersey statewide virtual job fair to connect job seekers and employers via a virtual hiring platform. *Virtual* job fairs have proven to be a popular option that enables people to interview live with human resources recruiters and hiring managers. The statewide New Jersey virtual job fair hosted many employers that were recruiting live via the fair's virtual platform. You could log in from your home and interview live with many companies. All you had to do was register for free by clicking on the link that the organization provided. What is becoming our motto? "Free is good!" There are so many free available resources out there; avail yourself of them.

The event ran from 5:00 pm to 8:00 pm. Candidates were interviewed live by hiring managers. They were asked to *upload* their résumé, dress in *business attire*, and *chat live*.

- Certain words are highlighted in italics—*virtual; upload; business attire;* and *chat live*. Would you be ready to jump in feet first to a virtual hiring fair? You want to be ready when an online interview happens, whether through a large group setting like the one described above or a one-to-one situation.
- Discover job fairs in your area.
- Start a systematic way to set up your job searches.

Checklist #3

Practice video interview

		Status?	Notes to self
1	Make a list of your strong personal characteristics.		
2	Make a list of the areas that you need to work on? Write down how you plan to work on these.		
3	Describe how the "you" of today is different from the "you" of a decade ago.		
4	Make a list of your skill sets acquired from other jobs.		
5	Based on the *Occupational Outlook Handbook*, identify the skill sets required for the jobs you will be applying for, matched with your strengths.		
6	Identify and register for the job fairs you have found, either online or in your area.		
7	Have your timelines been realistic?		
8	Are you maintaining your calendar of accountability?		
9	Check off those people on your contact list whom you have already reached out to.		
10			

11			
12			

Section 4. The Campaign Begins!

You did it before; you can do it again!

For every person searching for a job, there is a basic sequence of activities:

- ✓ The research
- ✓ The résumé
- ✓ The cover letter, which is optional depending on the situation
- ✓ The interviews (for some jobs there could be a demonstration piece or a performance piece, but that is only for certain fields)
- ✓ The follow-up plan, including the thank-you letter (as you will see later, you are not done when you walk out of the interview)

As we go through the book, we will provide details for each step. If we dot all the i's and cross all the t's in advance, the process will go as planned.

The Research

By now you should be familiar with the job-hunting sites and the *Occupational Outlook Handbook* cited in section 2.

- What strategy did you use to work through the job-hunting sites? Which ones have you found that can be beneficial to you?
- In the *Occupational Outlook Handbook*, you found there are twenty-five occupation groups and 808 occupations. How did you begin your search? By occupation group?

Let's say that you opened "Management." There you saw twenty-four sub-categories each with a job summary, entry-level education, and median pay.

- Under "Management," let's say that you have experience in administration. Let's open "Administrative Services Manager." Now we get detailed information—"What They Do," "Work Environment," "How to Become One," "Pay," "Job Outlook," "State & Area Data," "Similar Occupations," and "More Information." You can see how each category provides you with different and necessary information for your job hunt.

- Companies have been known to create their own unique job titles. If the title in the ad is not found in the *Occupational Outlook Handbook*, find the one that most closely resembles the description in the ad.

- By now you should have discovered what a valuable resource the *Occupational Outlook Handbook* is.

- Advance your education. Have you visited TED Talks and Khan Academy, or started taking a MOOC? If not, do so now.

- Research professional associations. You should find professional associations in your field, a field related to your current area, or the new field that you are interested in. Join the most beneficial and go to its meetings. Perhaps you think, "I went to one once, and it was boring." That is so not the point. Professional associations can prove to be an excellent way to network as well as to stay contemporary in your field. Being a member also looks good on a résumé because it says that you support the field that you want to work in.

- Build your network. Go to as many meetings and networking events as you can. Have your personal business cards with you. Personal business cards are valuable tools when you network as well as when you go on your interviews.

- Keep the card simple—name, email, and cell number.
- If you have a degree and the job you are looking for usually requires a degree, add it after your name.
- The advantages of a personal business card are (1) your card in the hands of interviewers is a reminder of you and your professionalism, and (2) if the interviewer does not hand you a card, they will once you present yours. If not, ask for a card.
- When you go to meetings or networking events, be open; be pleasant. Go up to a group casually and simply say, "May I join you?" Listen and learn. If anyone seems interested in helping your job hunt, follow up. Write notes and reminders on the back of the person's business card.
- Thoroughly research the companies that you are applying to. Know the company's key competition. For example, if you are interviewing at the headquarters of a restaurant chain, know which restaurants are their main competition so you can go in prepared. Also, know what other companies the parent company owns. You don't want to go in and say, "I really hate seafood" if the chain's biggest moneymaker is their seafood division. And by the way, don't *hate* anything.

The Résumé

Regarding your résumé, you will definitely need to dust it off and carefully update it. I interviewed many people in decision-making positions and *all* of them agreed that the résumé is *the* most important component of this process. The résumé does not get you the job; it gets you the interview, and its goal is to create interest in *you*.

You might also hear the term *CV*, which stands for curriculum vita. The primary difference between a résumé and a CV lies in its length. Where the résumé is typically one or two pages long and presents the highlights of your career, the CV presents *all* your work and academic career as well as your professional activities such as presentations and publications.

Modernize your résumé:

- Make your logo look modern. There is no need to reinvent the wheel; for example, Word provides many attractive résumé templates.

The contact information in your logo should include your name, email address, and cell number. Do not include your physical address.

- Don't let your email age you. No AOL or Yahoo. It is easy and free to create a Gmail account. You may want to create a separate email account for your job applications and correspondence so that responses are not lost amid Groupon offers.
- If you have a digital portfolio, you can include the URL in your logo. The link can also be put at the end of the résumé, stating, "To see my portfolio, please go to..."
- Include your LinkedIn profile. Make sure that your profile is up to date and reflects your intended direction.
- Use a modern font—Arial, Calibri, or Tahoma.
- Stick to one font throughout.
- Rather than an objectives statement, simply state the job you are applying for.

- The descriptive paragraphs in your résumé will relate to the job you are applying for.
- Use action keywords. (See appendix A for sample action words.)
- Eliminate "responsible for…" Emphasize achievements and quantifiable results.
- Save your résumé as a PDF. This way it will maintain the formatting you intend.
- Use a filename that clearly shows that the résumé is from you. Put your name up front in the filename—for example, "Raymond.Adams Resume". Make everything as easy as possible for the interviewer. Separate yourself from the pack.
- Do not include "references available upon request." It is expected that you can find references.

The key to any successful job campaign is to lay out the steps in a logical, chronological way. To do this, the sequence that we will follow for many of our activities is research, gather, sequence, and hit the mark. Let's start this process with the résumé:

- **Research**. Have vision and scope—vision to determine what the characteristics of that job are, and scope to discover what the company is looking for in an applicant.
- **Gather**. We will compile our achievements. For the résumé that means creating an entire list of your experiences, full time, part time, and volunteer.
- **Sequence**. From the master list we will describe ten to twelve of your greatest accomplishments. From these ten to twelve we will select the five to six that are most closely aligned to this job.

- **Hit the mark**. Fourth, we will package the materials in the résumé to best reflect your accomplishments.

Consider this first résumé as the *core* résumé, the template. Our goal is to have a well-written core résumé that states the basic facts; then we will customize it in order to highlight your accomplishments and target the résumé for that particular job. The core résumé will be longer than the custom version used in response to specific jobs. It should be complete, a template from which to draw.

We will use the terms *"core résumé"*, *"core cover letter"*, and *"core thank-you letter"* frequently. These are the basic templates from which you will be customizing your résumé, cover letter, and thank-you letter for each specific job.

- Write a functional résumé, not a chronological résumé. A chronological résumé reads like a grocery list and is boring. A functional résumé tells the reader what you have accomplished—what you *did* on that job. Use action words. If you need some ideas, a list can be found at the end of the book.
- When presenting your education, list the highest degree first. People remember what they see first, so start the section with a bang. The same is true for licenses and certifications. If you have a certificate and an advanced certificate, list the more advanced certificate first. If you have a master's degree and a bachelor's degree, list the master's degree first. That is what people will remember.
- Avoid using acronyms. Not everyone might know what CET or HSU stands for. People in the engineering field would know that CET stands for certified engineering technician. However, is HSU Humboldt State University? Hardin-Simmons University? Henderson State Uni-

versity? Avoid confusion. Spell the name out the first time you use it, followed immediately by the acronym in parentheses—for example, "When I attended Humboldt State University (HSU)…" Then you can use HSU throughout the rest of the document, once you let the reader know what it stands for.

- Use action words when describing what you have done in your functional résumé. Help the reader to envision your accomplishments on that job that relate to this new job. A list of sample action words is provided in appendix A.
- Proofread. Proofread. Proofread. Then give it to a family member or friend who has excellent proofreading skills and have them read it. You only get one chance to make a good first impression. There is no "re-do" in this.

Before we start assembling your materials, it is important that we understand the landscape—the vision, which is the plan that moves us toward our goal and the scope, all the assorted components that make our steps to success happen.

- The key to building a professional-looking résumé is in the *planning*, not in the writing. The story has already been written. Now it is your job to present the material in a relatable, attractive, and easy-to-understand manner.
- What skills and abilities are valued in the industry to which you are applying? If you have any questions, the *Occupational Outlook Handbook* will be helpful here.
- What does the job ad state that the company is looking for in an applicant? Remember— the ad is the company's wish list. Will anyone meet all eight or ten items

listed? Probably not. However, it is your job to address each of the key words in the ad and show how your strengths apply to that job.

- This is not to be confused with required criteria. If the job states that an applicant must have a specific requirement and you don't have it, don't apply for that job. That sounds so obvious but once I was interviewing candidates and the job specifically said, "Must have a Bachelor's Degree". A person wrote that she was currently in community college but would soon attend a four-year college. She planned to have her degree in three years. We wrote her a polite thank-you letter while shaking our heads. Applying for a job if you don't have the requirements could eliminate you for future consideration for another job in that company.

- Before assembling anything, analyze the position from many different angles and perspectives so that you can give them what they are looking for.

- Make a list of the types of industries to which you will be applying. What are the common characteristics? How do the industries differ?

- Put yourself in the place of the interviewer. What qualifications would you look for in an applicant for this position?

- Another consideration is determining your "brand," a term in common use today to describe the image that you want to present. What image—your brand—do you want to convey to the reader through your résumé?

If you do this correctly, it will allow the interviewer to visualize what you have done in the most positive light possible.

Once you have a feel for what your industry is looking for, you can start gathering—pulling together examples of your accomplishments that match what they are looking for. Visualize a trunk filled with examples of your best work experiences. For each interview, ask yourself, "What's in the trunk that I can pull from to get this particular job?"

- The first step is to make a master list of every full-time job, every part-time job, and every volunteer position or intern job you have had. Right now, we are just brainstorming. Write down all your accomplishments for each job. Put everything down. Do not filter anything out.

- It is always easier to scale down than to look at a blank page and have to write new material. Keep the master list of accomplishments saved as a template—this way you can pull out your different accomplishments as they relate to the job requirements.

- From the master list, extract accomplishments from your previous jobs that are most related to this job.

- Narrow this list to your top ten to twelve accomplishments.

- Narrow that list down again to the best five or six for the job for which you are applying.

- Remember, we are writing a functional résumé, so we need five or six paragraphs detailing your accomplishments, with specific examples. These are the jobs that gave you a sense of accomplishment. Prioritize which jobs you could discuss with a sense of pride. Use action words to describe those jobs.

- Some people say to me, "But I haven't done anything" and I always reply "You have not gotten to be the age you are without having done *something*." So, let's take a deeper look and start compiling your accomplishments.

- As you select each example of your work experience to include in the résumé, ask yourself, "What do my experiences have to do with this job?" It might not be the same industry; however, the skill sets could be the same or transferable.
- Ordinarily, you should leave out your hobbies. However, if your hobby is in line with the job, then include it. For example, if running is your hobby and you are interviewing at Nike or New Balance, this would be appropriate.
- If you have received any awards or recognitions, relate them to the job, if they apply.
- Match your accomplishments to the position. If the ad did not give a job description, you can always find key words for that job or a similar one in the *Occupational Outlook Handbook*.

Your résumé should answer the key questions "Why me?" "Why should they hire me?" "What makes me stand out from the rest of the applicants?" and "What will I bring to the job? To the company?" The résumé generates the interest in *you*.

All you have to do is follow the directions. There is no creative writing here. There is nothing new. You are writing about what you have done in the past.

Because there are over sixteen million websites dedicated to "functional résumés," be specific in your search, and you will find examples that work for you.

If you don't blow your own horn...

Checklist #4

The research and the résumé

		Status?	Notes to self
1	Did you do a deep dive into the field you are interested in?		
2	Are you current in the knowledge, skills, and language appropriate to the field you are looking at?		
3	Have you started to network?		
4	Have you placed your order for your business cards?		
5	Have you written your core functional résumé, noting places where you can customize your achievements for each individual job?		
6	Are you able to identify key words in an ad, to relate them to your strengths?		
7	Make a list of all your accomplishments from every job.		
8	Narrow it down to your top ten to twelve accomplishments.		
9	Narrow it down again, to the five to six for that particular job.		
10	Now you should be able to demonstrate why you would be the best candidate for the job.		

11	Does the résumé look attractive? First impressions are so important.		
12	Do you have a proofreader in place?		
13	Have your timelines been realistic?		
14	Are you maintaining your calendar of accountability?		
15			
16			
17			

The Cover Letter

Just as you have a core résumé, you will have a core cover letter. Like résumés, there are millions of examples of cover letters (this is a generic term that covers emails as well). The cover letter is your opportunity to custom-tailor interest in you by highlighting your assets from your résumé.

Historically, cover letters began when people would mail a résumé to an employer. It was considered poor form to just stick a résumé in an envelope. A cover letter softened the message and served as an introduction. Recently, I interviewed people in hiring positions in large and small companies and learned that, today, many in hiring positions question its worth.

If it doesn't add, it detracts.

- The cover letter could be a liability if you go in a direction that the interviewer wasn't expecting or if you don't build on the points raised in your résumé.

- You need to be purpose driven when you submit a cover letter. You are asking for more of the interviewer's time. Make the letter be an enhancement to the résumé.
- The cover letter should include information that the interviewer can act on.
- If you are not a good writer, think about whether you should submit a cover letter. If you have typos; bad grammar, spelling, and punctuation; or bad sentence structure; or if your letter is boring, it goes against the inevitable comments that people make in their résumés—"I am detail oriented" and "I have strong written communication skills." Sometimes less is best. Remember: if it doesn't add, it subtracts; if it doesn't add value, it detracts from the goal.
- If the résumé and the cover letter are not uploaded together, the interviewer may never see the cover letter.
- If you choose to include a cover letter, be sure to include:
  ✓ why you want this job,
  ✓ why you are qualified for this job,
  ✓ why you would excel at this job, and
  ✓ what you can contribute to the organization.
- If you do not send your cover email with your logo, be sure to include your contact information. For example, a usual place to put your email and cell phone number are at the bottom, below your signature.
- If you have created a digital portfolio (which we will discuss in detail in chapter 3), refer the reader to your digital portfolio's URL in the letter and explain what the reader will find in the portfolio—your résumé, samples of your accomplishments related to that position, certificates, and other relevant information.

The Thank-You Letter

Just as you have a core résumé and a core cover letter, you will have a core thank-you letter. If you have not heard about the importance of the follow-up thank-you letter, now is the time. When I searched "Interview Thank-You Email," there were over four hundred million hits.

The importance of a thank-you letter/email cannot be underestimated. In addition to thanking the person for their time, it gives you one more opportunity to remind the interviewer about you and your value, and to recap key points from the interview.

- Many employers believe that a thank-you email is much more important than a cover letter, especially when you are interviewing in a relationship-oriented industry such as insurance, accounting, and banking.
- Your letter should communicate interest in the position, show politeness, and recap a level of understanding of what was discussed during the interview. It must be timely.
- It is also an opportunity to clear up a response to an interview question. If you are not sure if you landed the punch in the interview, write that you have reflected on what was said and what your decision was. Leverage information gathered during the interview to your advantage.
- Your thank-you email should demonstrate that you have the competencies required to be successful at this job. These short bursts of adding a bit more can be impactful.

Think about your brand the whole way through.

In your thank-you letter, include:

- ✓ "thank you for the meeting,"
- ✓ why you are qualified for this job,
- ✓ why you would excel at this job,
- ✓ why you are sure that you can contribute to the organization,
- ✓ "looking forward to hearing from you soon!"

Social Media

- Appraise your Facebook page with a critical eye. If you think that a prospective employer won't look for your Facebook page, you are mistaken. Take down any pictures or other materials that might work against you during the job hunt.
- Do the same for *all* your other social media accounts.
- Make sure that your LinkedIn account is up-to-date and shows relevancy to your job hunt and the direction of your search.

The cover letter, the thank-you letter, and social media

		Status?	Notes to self
1	Have you written your core cover letter, noting places where you can customize the body for each individual job?		
2	Because cover letters are optional in many situations (especially with electronic transmission), look at your cover letter with a critical eye—if it doesn't add, it detracts.		
3	Have you written your core thank-you letter, noting places where you can customize the body for each individual job?		
4	Has your thank-you letter built a relationship between you and the interviewer(s)?		
5	Did your letter recap what was discussed and clear up any ambiguities?		
6	The thank-you letter is another opportunity to show that you are the best candidate for the job.		
7	Have you reviewed your social media account through the eyes of a future employer?		

8	Have your timelines been realistic?		
9	Are you maintaining your calendar of accountability?		
10			
11			
12			

Preparing for the Interview

One area in which everyone needs practice is the interview. It is not something that we do frequently or that we look forward to, and it is one of the things in life in which there is no "do-over." You only get one chance to make a good first impression, so make it count.

When I searched "Interview Hints and Tips," there were 16.9 million hits. Now, we don't expect you to read all of them; however, as you visit sites you will see that certain key points keep recurring:

- Review and evaluate the critiques that have people have given you in the past. Maybe they are right. Are you wordy? Interviewers do not want "blah, blah, blah." They want an elevator pitch—two to three minutes. Hit the key points. On the other hand, is talking to you like pulling teeth? During the interview you will be asked to talk about a topic that no one knows more about than you do—yourself. Sell yourself in the best possible light.
- Do you tend to say "you know" and "like" a lot when you get nervous? Work on eliminating those phrases.
- Learn to pause. It will help you gather your thoughts. Even if you have a ready answer, a thoughtful pause will make it look as if you are thinking about it.

- Phase one—practice *out loud* in front of the mirror. You will certainly feel funny—at first. However, the answers need to come out seamlessly. Also, you need to look pleasant, positive, comfortable, and confident.
- Phase two—graduate to grabbing family members and friends as your audience, and have them go through practice interviews.
- Then we will be ready for phase three—turning you loose on the key players—the interviewers with the jobs.

Possible Problem Areas

Anticipate what problems could arise and be ready for them. What are problem areas that you expect to come up? For example, "Why was your last job at a lower level than the one before?" Sticking your head in the sand or thinking that they won't notice is not the solution. Be prepared. Write down a list of those questions along with honest, succinct answers.

- Make a list of questions that you would hate to be asked—and have positive responses ready.
- There is a term called "handling objections." Again, anticipate any objections that the interviewer may raise and have positive responses ready.

For example, if the interviewer says, "You don't have familiarity with the XYZ system" and you have experience with the ABC system, stress equivalency. You could say, "They are both point-of-sale software, and I have had success using the ABC system, which is similar to the XYZ. I'm sure that I can quickly transfer my knowledge of the ABC to the XYZ." Turn a negative into a positive.

- The interviewer will invariably ask, "Do you have any questions?" Be prepared. Have thoughtful questions about the job ready to ask the interviewer about the position and about the company. This is not the time to discuss benefits such as "How many sick days?" or "How much vacation?" Your questions could be about the direction of the company in the next five years and the biggest opportunities facing the company and the department right now. Do not leave without asking what the next steps in the interview process will be.
- There could be sensitive questions. For example, if the interviewer says, "This job is below your abilities," you could reply, "My previous experience will serve me well in this job and contribute to the job and the company."
- Another common question is, "How much are you looking for?" Don't walk in unprepared. If you did your homework you should know what the range is. Get *them* to tell *you* the salary range. (You don't want to underestimate or overestimate the range.)
- Where do you see yourself five years from now? "I plan to continue contributing to the company." Do not be cute and say "In your job". They will say, "Thank you… Next…"

Preparing for a Phone Interview

Today many companies use the phone interview as the first screening device. Typically, this is a screening mechanism to save hiring managers time.

- They may review what is on your résumé and your salary history.
- They may ask why you applied.

- It is perfectly reasonable to ask human resources about the goals of each interview.
- Do your homework. Be prepared. See if you can get the name of the interviewer and look him/her up on LinkedIn and YouTube. If you have a network, ask if anyone knows the interviewer or has current information about the company. This will help make the interview go more smoothly and also shows your interest in the job. Companies like to make offers to people who they think have a real interest in the job.

The human resources department may take the first step in "feeling out" applicants by engaging in a phone interview. Regardless of whether it is the HR department or the person who is doing the hiring, do the following:

- Be prepared for the phone call.
- Find a quiet place.
- Make sure that you cell phone is fully charged.
- Have all of your paperwork in front of you (e.g. the job ad, your cover letter, your résumé, and any other relevant correspondence).
- Use your ear buds in order to have your hands free to take notes and look through your papers.
- Smile. A smile on your face can be heard in a phone call.
- Keep your enthusiasm level high. Stand up. When you sit down your energy level goes down.
- Keep your tone formal. This is still an interview, not a phone chat.

Preparing for a Video Interview

Part of the interview process will probably be a video interview. If you have never participated in a video-conference, have a friend or family member set up several video-conferences so you become confident being part of an online meeting.

- There are many free video-conferencing tools. One well-known company is Zoom. When someone sets up a Zoom conference, as the participant all you have to do is click on the link that you were sent or copy the URL or type in the meeting URL.
- Get comfortable. Practice helps you to become familiar with the volume on the microphone, the angle of the camera, and other features. One practice session is not enough.
- Be sure to maintain eye contact with the other person throughout the video. Video eye contact means looking at the camera so that the interviewer is looking in your eyes. Try to position the camera at eye level so you don't look like you're staring up at the ceiling. Practice so that you don't look like a deer in the headlights.
- If you are going to conduct the video interview on your cell phone, buy a cell phone stand. It is so inexpensive. You cannot hold a cell phone steady for a long period of time. Put the phone and stand on a stack of books so that you are looking straight out at the phone/camera.
- Dress as if you were going to a face-to-face interview.
- Look for the most attractive background in your house. In particular, you don't want to show open closet doors, bathroom doors, or piles of papers on the floor. Go for a neutral background.

- Make sure you have privacy, with no one walking around in your shot.
- Also practice with lighting. There are many websites that provide hints and tips. Basically, you want an even lighting across your face without shadows.
- Be sure to turn the ringer off your cell and landline phones. Better yet, unless you are using your cell phone for the interview, put it in another room so you are not tempted to look at it. Anything that is controllable should be. This meeting is your main focus right now.
- Interviewers do not want to waste valuable interview time while you fiddle around, yell "Can you hear me?," or wave your arms around frantically. Practice is essential here. Otherwise, they are thinking, "Thank you… Next…"

The Follow-Up Plan

The importance of this part of the process should not be underestimated. You cannot just sit and wait for the interviewer to call you. You have to be proactive, especially if you really, *really* want that job.

- Earlier, we discussed a key component of the follow-up plan—the core thank-you letter/email. You should have it written by now.
- Some people say, "I'm not good with names." You don't have to be; you only have to be good with names for the five minutes you are writing the thank-you letter. The business cards you were given during the interviews are your resources to get the names and titles correct.
- Update all pertinent information in your file for that particular company.

- In your calendar, note dates for follow-up phone calls and/or emails.
- Have you kept in touch with your mentors? Never burn your bridges behind you. You never know who knows whom. In the technology industry there was an old expression when we would go to technology conferences: the names and faces stay the same; only the booths change.

Let's pull together all the resources we need for our plan of attack. Check your accomplishments:

✓ Do I honestly feel that I did a deep dive into the field? What other job titles are out there that are similar to what I did?

✓ Am I current in my knowledge, skills, and language appropriate to the field I am looking at?

✓ Have I had personal business cards printed?

✓ Do I have a core résumé, with sections noted for updating by specific job?

✓ Do I have a core cover letter, with sections noted for customization?

✓ Do I have a core thank-you letter ready, with sections noted for customization?

✓ Have I honed my interview skills in practice phone interviews?

✓ Have I honed my interview skills in practice video interviews?

Preparing for the interviews and the follow-up plan

		Status?	Notes to self
1	Have you reviewed and evaluated critiques from others in order to improve your interview presentation?		
2	Have you listed your annoying speaking habits and worked on eliminating them?		
3	Have you practiced an interview in front of a mirror out loud?		
4	Have you practiced an interview with friends or family?		
5	Have you made a list of questions you would hate to be asked?		
6	Have you prepared responses for possible problem or sensitive questions?		
7	Have you prepared questions for the "Do you have any questions?" question?		
8	Have you participated in a few practice phone interviews? Were you happy with the results?		

9	Have you participated in a few practice video interviews? Were you happy with the results?		
10	What else have you done to prepare for the interviews?		
11	Have you written the procedures for your follow-up plan?		
12	Have your timelines been realistic?		
13	Are you maintaining your calendar of accountability?		
14			
15			
16			

Chapter 2

Getting the Job

In this section you are pulling together all the resources you have gathered into a logical chronological sequence. You submitted your package, and you have been asked to come in for an in-person interview. Now you get to showcase yourself: "Before the Interview," "Getting in the Mind-Set," "During the Interview," and "Following Up."

Section 1. Before the Interview

- Before you go on an interview, review all of your research about that company, the parent company, any subsidiaries, the competition, and the industry as a whole.
- Do your homework. Google the interviewers to see if they made any presentations. Know your audience.
- Prepare your outfit for the interview; dress for the type of industry you are interviewing for. You might be interviewed in a small room; therefore, do not wear perfume or cologne.
- Practice, practice, practice. Being well-prepared is far different from sounding "canned."
- Review each detail on your résumé.
- Make note of the name of your first point of contact. That person is your key for future interviews.
- Remember to bring *at least* two complete sets of all important paperwork printed on good stock paper, not plain copy paper. Write talking points on your copy. Nobody wants to stop the rhythm of the interview by looking things up on the computer. Also, if the interviewer

invites you to meet with other decision makers, you're ready.

- Map your route, especially if you have never been to that area before. Remember Murphy's Law—"If it can go wrong, it will go wrong," and I always add, "and it will happen to you." It is never good to start an interview with frustrated interviewers. It can be overcome, but if the job is one that requires attention to detail, this is not a good start. It's all part of the screening process.

- If you get to the interview on time, you're late. Get there early. There is always a place to go for coffee. Better you know that you are where you should be than to run in, all stressed. Also, what if the last person finished early or never showed up and they are looking for you? Being late for an interview tells the interviewer that you will be late for work.

Checklist #7

Before the interview

		Status?	Notes to self
1	Review all your research before you go on the interview.		
2	Lay out your outfit in advance of the interview, in case any modifications have to be made.		
3	Keep practicing right up to the time of the interview.		
4	Take several sets of all important paperwork with you.		
5	Do not be on time—be early!		
6	Whether you are driving or taking public transportation, be prepared for any eventuality.		
7	Have your timelines been realistic?		
8	Are you maintaining your calendar of accountability?		
9			
10			
11			

Section 2. The Interview – Getting in the Mind-set

- Many people believe that the interviewer's decision is made in the first five minutes. You want to create credibility, believability, and value.

- However, the interview really begins as soon as you enter the building. Be pleasant and professional to everyone! Make eye contact with everyone! Be courteous to the receptionist. Do not underestimate the influence of the administrative staff. Follow directions about where to park and how to gain admission to the building. The last thing you want to do is accidentally park in the President's spot.

- Go in and stay positive. Your mind-set going in is key. At the end of the interview, the interviewer will feel a level of trust about you: absolute trust (rare on a first meeting); high confidence; confidence (the most common); or no confidence at all (possible if you don't handle things well). You know which level you want to aim for from the moment you walk in the door. "Be yourself; everyone else is already taken."—Oscar Wilde

- The best advice that anyone ever gave me is, "Just be yourself." Whether it is going up to a group of strangers at a networking event or meeting the interviewer, we all get butterflies. Just be yourself—with an extra touch of enthusiasm. Be the best you that you can be. No one can ask for anything more.

- Envision that it's already your job. This advice really works: when you are sitting in the interview, see your job right behind the interviewer. The only thing standing between you and your job is the interviewer. So, your job is to convince them that you are the right person for the job. Someone has to get the job—make it you.

- Be positive. Be pleasant. Do not talk negatively about your previous job. No matter how angry you may be about a previous situation, that's in the past. Look forward, not backward. You want to be seen as a team player, not a whiner and complainer.

- Demonstrate to the interviewer that you have vision and scope, vision because you don't just see the here and now; you can see your future with the company and scope because you see how the job that you are interviewing for fits into the overall objectives of the company.

- Put yourself on the same side as the interviewer. The interviewer is not your adversary. They are trying to find a candidate; you are trying to find a job. You are both on the same team.

- Think positively. Because you remembered to bring extra copies of your paperwork with you, when the interviewer says, "While you're here, I'd like you to meet someone else," that's no problem! You're ready!

- Send up a trial balloon—do not go for the job you really, *really* want first. Practice. Iron out the kinks. Save your dream job for interview number two.

- Lower your stress level by saying to yourself, "This will be over in an hour." That's how long you have to dazzle them.

The interview—getting in the mindset

		Status?	Notes to self
1	Think about the impression that you want to make in the first five minutes.		
2	Remember that the interview starts as soon as you walk into the building. Be pleasant and professional to everyone.		
3	Stay positive throughout.		
4	Just be yourself—with an extra touch of enthusiasm.		
5	This is your job. Now, convince the interviewer of that fact.		
6	Find positive things to say about your previous jobs.		
7	All the research you have done will come in handy here. Show your vision and scope.		
8	Remember that the interviewer and you are on the same team.		
9	Did you go on a practice interview first?		
10	After you meet with one person, you're ready to meet with more people because you have brought extra copies.		
11	Have your timelines been realistic?		

12	Are you maintaining your calendar of accountability?		
13			
14			
15			

Section 3. During the Interview

- Be in control of the interview. You might say, "How am I in control? The interviewer is the one with the job." What that means is that it is your job to keep the tempo of the interview lively and not have dead spots. If a key point that you wanted to make has not been covered, segue in a logical way from the current topic to the one you want to discuss.

- Listen closely to the interviewer. What you *think* they were asking might not be what they were looking for. If you don't understand the question, ask for clarification or for an example. You want your response to be intelligent and to match the question.

- Don't talk too much. Answer the question and do not go off on a tangent. Give the interviewer a chance to continue the conversation. There is an expression in marketing called "talking through the close." Sometimes you could inadvertently say too much and open a door that does not need to be opened.

- Maximize the "Tell me about yourself" question. Invariably, that will be one of the first questions. It is an ice-breaker. Have a presentation ready that focuses on your professional skills—short and to the point, enhanced with anecdotes that specifically illustrate how you applied each one. "The three most important things that I would like you to know about me are A, B, and C. When I was working for XYZ Company, I did A." Then go on to B, with an anecdote; then C, with a related anecdote. This is what we mean by "take control of the interview." Take the conversation in the direction in which *you* wish to steer it for your benefit.

- Highlight your achievements. Go in with "I am qualified by...," "My capabilities are...," and "I have accomplished..."
- Integrate your best characteristics with the job requirements.
- Be prepared for this common question: "What strengths would you bring to the company that would enhance the department and the company as a whole?"
- Give concrete examples: Not "I'm a hard worker" but an example that typifies an outstanding job that you did.
- I once heard the expression "Learn how to tap dance." In the interview situation, it means learn to fill in the dead spots. If the conversation seems to be lagging, pick it up.
- Ask relevant questions. Find interesting things to add in order to sell yourself.
- There will probably be a behavior-based question: "Tell us about a situation that did not go well for you, and, if you could do it all over again, what would you do differently?" Also, be prepared for a situational question about that particular industry: "We are having a problem in a specific area. How would you handle it?"
- Know your audience. Performers say that they learn to "read" the crowd they're performing to. They know when the crowd is with them or when they've lost them.

Develop that skill in yourself. If you find conversation waning, spark interest.

- Read the interviewer's body language. For example, if you notice an interviewer's eyes glazing over, know to change tactics.
- Discern the interviewer's tempo. If they seem laid back, don't come in talking at a hundred miles per hour. If they are bubbly and lively, step up your game. Match the interviewer's level.
- If you don't know about a topic, politely say so. The interviewer knows the industry and can spot a phony a mile away.
- If you don't know the specific answer to a question, say, "I don't know, but I'll get back to you." This is a perfect opportunity for you to send a follow-up thank-you email with the answer to what you said you'd look up.
- Never talk about money, sick days, or vacation days. Do not accept or reject the job in the room. Think about it.
- Toward the end of the interview, you may be asked, "What question did you think that we were going to ask that we didn't? And if we ask it now, how would you answer it?" Have a question and a response ready.
- In your closing remarks, repeat back to the interviewer key points they made about the job and add to it— showing how you hit those marks.
- When the interviewer stands up and extends their hand, the interview is over. When you shake hands, hold eye contact and add a closing statement, such as "Thank you for your time. I look forward to joining the team."
- When the interview is over, to help with future interviews, ask yourself what went well, what went wrong, and what changes you could make for the next inter-

view. Listen to your intuition. You know what went well and what did not. Do this as soon as you leave the interview so you do not forget key points. A few days later might be too late if you have gone on several interviews.

- As part of the hiring process, some companies may ask you to take an assessment test, give you a case study to complete, or request that you demonstrate a job-related skill. Job assessments, based on job level and field, could be job aptitude, basic skills assessment, soft skills assessment, or tests giving insight to a candidate's personality and/or ethics. These tests can determine how the candidate might fit in culture of the organization. In addition, these types of tests offer the company a quick way to assess the job readiness of a candidate in a range of jobs. These is really no way to study for them.

Checklist #9

During the interview

		Status?	Notes to self
1	Have you thought about techniques you could use to keep the conversation flowing and ways to fill in the dead spots?		
2	Practice the skill of listening closely.		
3	Answer the questions directly and stay on topic.		
4	Did you prepare for the "Tell me about yourself" question?		
5	Itemize all the points that you want to be sure to make.		
6	Did the interviewer ask any behavior-based questions?		
7	Do you feel that the interviewer and you were on the same page?		
8	How would you explain the interviewer's style?		
9	Did the interviewer ask any question for which you were not prepared? Write them down to prepare for the next interview.		
10	Did you leave on a high note with a positive closing/exit statement?		

11	Analyze in detail what went well and what did not so you are ready for the next interview.		
12	Have your timelines been realistic?		
13	Are you maintaining your calendar of accountability?		
14			
15			
16			

Section 4. Following Up

As we said, the thank-you letter is about building relationships. Remember—you and the interviewer are on the same side.

- As soon as the interview is over, make notes on the back of the interviewer's business card for reference.
- If the interviewer had a unisex first name, such as Riley, Peyton, or Lesley, write "Mr." or "Ms." on the card so that you get the salutation right in the thank-you letter.
- Send a thank-you email before the end of the next business day. Here is where having a well-written thank-you letter already prepared will make the process much easier. Be sure to customize your core thank-you letter specifically to the recipient.
- Pick up on clues learned during the interview. For example, if the interviewer tells you that they have three more people to interview and they should be done by Friday, time is of the essence. Send a well-written thank-you email that day.

- Customize each letter. Make the thank-you letter specific to the job and reinforce why you are the best candidate.
- Proofread the thank-you letter closely. Spell the name and company correctly. Then double-check it. Do not just cut and paste from letter to letter. You might have left something from the last letter in this new one. The last thing you want to do is, if you were interviewed by Mary Smith, to accidentally address it to Mr. Smith because your cut-and-paste skills were not up to par.
- If the interviewer requested additional information or documents such as an application form or references, do it and confirm in your thank-you letter that you have done as instructed.
- Scan the interviewer's business card and save it electronically as part of that job's complete digital folder. When you are called back for the second and third interviews, you have to step up your game. Interviews numbers two and three won't be the "same old, same old":
- The company has narrowed down the field. Now the expectations of your performance will be on a higher level. Do more research. Be even more prepared about the job, the company, and the competition. Analyze the first interview and pick up on key points.
- What did you do well that caused you to be invited back? What will you do differently the next time?
- The second and subsequent interviews could consist of a panel of people. Be sure to consistently make eye contact with every person in the room or on the screen.
- Did you ask for the names of the people who will be interviewing you? Did you look them up? Can you determine who the decision makers will be?

- If you are asked for references, *ask* the people first, before giving their names and contact information. Also, make sure that their information is up to date—current job title and most recent phone number and email address.

Keep Up the Momentum

- Until you have the job offer in hand, keep up the job search momentum.
- Refer to the list of all the jobs that you have applied for so far. Is it as long as you'd hoped it would be? Have you been keeping an electronic folder for each one?
- Reach out to those interviewers whom you have not heard from about the status of the position. Email is usually preferred over voice mail.
- If you are not receiving any call-backs, why not? What can you do differently?

Checklist #10

Following up

		Status?	Notes to self
1	Make notes to yourself as soon as you can after the interview.		
2	Get the thank-you letter out by tomorrow.		
3	What hints and tips did you pick up on during the interview?		
4	Customize and proofread each thank-you note carefully. Does this letter help build a relationship with the interviewer?		
5	If the interviewer directs you to do something, do it right away and let them know that you did it in the thank-you letter.		
6	Did the interviewer give you any indication of time frames?		
7	Immediately scan all business cards and save them in the digital folder for that particular job. Business cards are one of the easiest things to misplace.		
8	Reach out to those you have not heard from about the status of the position. Don't just sit around and wait for them to call you.		

9	For the subsequent interviews, be even more prepared. Anticipate the difficult questions.		
10	Analyze why they called you back.		
11	Remember to make eye contact with everyone, whether it is a video or an in-person meeting.		
12	Find out who will be there; then determine who the decision makers are.		
13	Ask people before you give their names as references. Make sure that you have the most recent contact information.		
14	Until you get a position, what are you doing to keep up the momentum?		
15	If responses are slow in coming in, what can you do to change?		
16	Have your timelines been realistic?		
17	Are you maintaining your calendar of accountability?		
18			
19			
20			

Chapter 3

The Portfolio

Regardless of your walk of life or stage in your career, it is in your best interest to create a portfolio. Look at a portfolio as a collection of the best of your work experiences. Don't let the word "portfolio" sound daunting. Perhaps you think that portfolios are for "other people." Just think of a portfolio as a way to present yourself in the best possible light.

The focus of this book is about finding a job, and your portfolio can definitely be an asset in this area. Once you get the job, your portfolio will continue to be a valuable asset. There will be other circumstances when having an up-to-date, well-written portfolio will prove to be helpful. To demonstrate the importance of the portfolio, we have devoted an entire chapter to the topic, and we will analyze the different roles that portfolios can play along the employment journey.

Why should you create a portfolio? A portfolio is your opportunity to show your accomplishments to others. Your portfolio allows an employer to see your professionalism and how you are well suited for this job.

Section 1. When Is the Right Time for a Portfolio?

When might you need a portfolio? Any time is the right time to present your portfolio. Three examples along the employment timeline can be seen in:

- section 2 of this chapter, about looking for a job or beginning a career;
- section 3 of this chapter, about performance reviews; and

- section 4 of this chapter, about seeking to advance in one's career, whether that means moving to a new organization or staying in one's current one.

If you don't have a portfolio, let's build one. If you have had a portfolio for years, now is the time to review it and update it. The first time that you assemble your portfolio is the most time-consuming, and you might feel like you are groping in the dark. Once you get your portfolio set up and you are happy with the content, it is so simple to just add new material and keep it updated.

Remember the term "*chunklets*"? We are going to break this project down into manageable pieces. No one creates or updates a portfolio in one sitting. They step away, go back, re-examine it, and make changes through fresh eyes. A portfolio is always a work in progress.

Section 2. When You Are Looking for a Job or Beginning Your Career

Just like writing the résumé, the key to building a professional-looking portfolio is in the *planning*. The story has already been written. Now it is your job to present the material in an attractive and easy-to-follow manner. The key to any successful job campaign is in laying out the steps in a logical way, and we will follow the same sequence that we did for the résumé:

- **Research**. Have vision and scope: vision to determine what brand—what image—you want to convey to the reader through your portfolio, and scope to be sure to include the key elements that the reader will be looking for.
- **Gather**. Then we will compile all your accomplishments.

- **Sequence**. Next, we will narrow the examples down, specific to each job.
- **Hit the mark**. Fourth, we will package the materials in the portfolio to best reflect why you are the best candidate for the job.

Before we start assembling your portfolio, it is important that we understand the landscape—the plan that moves us toward our goal as well as all the assorted components that make our steps to success happen.

- The key to building a professional-looking portfolio is in the *planning*, not in the writing. You want to present your achievements in a logical, attractive, and easy-to-understand manner.
- Before assembling your portfolio, analyze the position from many different angles and perspectives so that you can give them what they are looking for.
- Put yourself in the place of the reader. What qualifications would you look for in an applicant for this position?
- With your portfolio, a key consideration is your "brand." What image—your brand—do you want your portfolio to convey?

Once you have a feel for what your industry is looking for, we can start gathering—pulling together examples of your accomplishments that match what they are looking for. Remember the analogy of the trunk filled with examples of your best work experiences? What accomplishments can you showcase to create your best portfolio?

- Use the master list that you created when you wrote your résumé to refresh your memory.

- Your functional résumé is the organizer. The portfolio is the place to showcase each accomplishment cited in the résumé. Include visuals as much as you can. People like pictures and color.

Narrow this list to your top ten to twelve accomplishments.

- Narrow that list down again to the best five or six for the job for which you are applying.
- If you have received any awards or recognitions, scan those documents as well.
- Some people are better at visually presenting their work than describing it in words. Use your graphic skills to enhance your portfolio.
- Here is where your scanning abilities come to the forefront. You could start one of your examples with the logo from the company or graphics that exemplify what you are talking about.

Your portfolio should help answer the key questions "Why you?" "Why should I hire *you*?" and "What makes you stand out from the rest of the applicants?" One way is to make sure that your portfolio is logical and easy to navigate. In addition, the reader should see a thread of continuity run through your work.

- First, your functional résumé has succinct paragraphs explaining your accomplishments in your various positions.
- Second, if you included a cover letter, it summarizes the accomplishments from your résumé as well as why you want this job, why you are qualified for this job, why you

would excel at this job, and what you can contribute to the organization.

- Third, the accomplishments from your résumé are explained in detail, with specific examples, in your portfolio. In essence, your achievements can be expanded upon in much greater detail in your portfolio.

The interviewer may read all your materials in detail or may not even open the portfolio. However, *you* know that you did everything right and that the portfolio will be beneficial in the future.

- ✓ Your goal is to showcase your skills and abilities, so make sure that each example included in your portfolio has a connection to the job for which you are applying.
- ✓ Although there is no set limit on the number of examples you can include, five to six is considered to be an adequate number.
- ✓ Ensure that each example is labeled clearly. Rather than "Database" or "Marketing Campaign," label it "Database That Reduced Shipping Costs" or "Marketing Campaign That Increased Clothing Sales."
- ✓ Relate each of your examples to particular components of that job. If the company wants "A", demonstrate how you have done "A." If the company wants "B", show how you have done "B."
- ✓ Avoid negative and wishy-washy phrases like "I hope," I think," and "I may." Be definitive.

The following story can help you select examples for your portfolio.

One of my graduate students, a carpentry teacher, worked in a high school where many of his students chose to go to work rather than to college. He had each of his seniors create a portfolio that contained examples of their best work from several different skill sets that a working carpenter would be required to have—photos and a description of a new kitchen that each student had installed as well as the plans the student had designed for that kitchen, the materials used for the job, the pricing for the job, and the invoice, as well as a résumé.

- Each student included examples in their portfolio that were specific to this industry, carpentry. These were young people just starting out, so the examples were rather basic. As a person grows in expertise in the field, the accomplishments will become more sophisticated, and the number of examples will increase.
- How can you transfer this example to documenting your accomplishments to the job you are going for?

For those of you who completed an internship or a co-op experience, include it in your portfolio. You were assigned to your placement because it tied in with your formal training.

- Pull together how (a) the placement tied together with (b) the training, which together relate to (c) the job for which you are interviewing. Show that thread of continuity.
- Describe accomplishments from your internship/co-op experience. The fact that you were not paid does not mean that you did not contribute to the organization. The job you did had value.

- Scan any evaluations or letters from people who super-vised you during your internship or co-op experience, and include them in the portfolio.
- Don't feel frustrated that "you don't have a lot" if this is the beginning of your work life. You cannot expect to have as many accomplishments as a person who has been working for decades.

Checklist #11

Looking for a job or beginning your career

		Status?	Notes to self
1	Go to your master list and extract ten to twelve accomplishments that are directly related to the job for which you are applying.		
2	Next, narrow the list down to five to six of the best examples from that list.		
3	Highlight each of those accomplishments.		
4	Use photos, graphics, and other visuals to highlight these accomplishments.		
5	Is each accomplishment clearly labeled?		
6	Does your portfolio answer the question "Why should I hire you?" If not, what do you need to change?		
7	What is the thread of continuity—the theme—running through your portfolio?		
8	What brand—your image—is portrayed in the portfolio?		
9	If you had an internship/co-op experience, did you relate it to key words in the job ad?		

10	Did you ask several people to review your portfolio?		
11	Did you evaluate and incorporate their feedback as appropriate?		
12	Have your timelines been realistic?		
13	Are you maintaining your calendar of accountability?		
14			
15			
16			

Section 3. When It Is Time for a Performance Review

A different focus of a portfolio occurs if you have an upcoming review. In this case, the criteria have already been defined, and it is your job to match up your accomplishments with the criteria. Hopefully, you have been keeping examples of your accomplishments in your portfolio since your last review. As with all portfolios, the story has already been written. All you have to do is to compile and present the material in an attractive and easy-to-follow manner. Recognize your strong points and demonstrate your strong points through your accomplishments. Enable your supervisor to see your accomplishments.

The steps are as follows:

- **Research**. Know the expectations. Have they changed since your last review?
- **Gather**. What does the job description state? Remember—it is totally acceptable to highlight activities that go beyond the job description. Address each of the key

points and show how you assumed responsibility and did more than the basic requirements.

Back to your "brand." What have you done to demonstrate professional growth since your last review? Can you demonstrate with specific examples how you worked on the suggestions for improvement (if there were any) from the last review? Overall, what image do you convey through your current portfolio?

- **Sequence**. It is your job to present the material in a logical, chronological, or functional sequence that highlights not only the job requirements but also those activities that are above and beyond. Put yourself in the place of the reader. What criteria are he or she looking for? Make them clearly stand out.
- **Hit the mark**. What examples in your portfolio make your accomplishments stand out? This is not the time to be subtle. Your promotion—or your retention—could be helped by a well-organized portfolio.

The key to any successful review is in laying out the materials in a logical way. This section will help you to do just that:

- At the beginning of your portfolio, provide a one-page summary sheet of your accomplishments since the last review. If there are many accomplishments, you can use a table or chart to keep the material simple and easy to understand. Then present the accomplishments in detail after the summary.
- Have you met all the expectations laid out for you? How did you document them?
- Be specific in your explanations. It is not enough to say "I increased..." or "I helped..." Show *how* you accomplished these activities.

- If there were any suggestions for improvement from the last review, document how you acted on them.
- Show how your accomplishments benefited the organization—not just "Here is what I did," but "Here is how what I did benefited the company."
- Have your goals for the next review period (year? quarter?) expressed in a clear and definite manner. Have you created and maintained a calendar for accountability that helps you meet your goals? If you cannot envision your accomplishments, how can anyone else?

You never know when an opportunity may arise. Volunteer and unpaid work have value. I have a friend who worked for a major telecommunications company that was a staunch supporter of the Special Olympics. He began as a volunteer at a booth at the Carnival of Fun. The people in charge saw how good he was, and he was put in charge of the entire Carnival of Fun, booths where the athletes could relax between events, play games, and win prizes.

This was a big responsibility and involved two-hundred-plus volunteers—getting people to volunteer for an entire Saturday, reminding them to show up, assigning people to booths, teaching the volunteers the games, making sure that each team had the materials to decorate its booth, distributing the prizes for the athletes that he had bought weeks before, making sure that lunch was provided for two hundred volunteers, troubleshooting problems all day long…and much more.

He put this on his functional résumé under Volunteer Activities. When interviewing for a higher position, he got the job, and the person who interviewed him told him that he was promoted because of his organizational ability. The interviewer said that my friend's face lit up during the interview when he was talking about the team effort of all those involved and the benefits of the Special Olympics to the athletes who participated. You never know when an opportunity could arise.

- Do you have volunteer experience that would showcase your unique skills and abilities?

Checklist #12

Performance review time

		Status?	Notes to self
1	In a performance review, it is highly acceptable to highlight activities that transcend the job description.		
2	Have you demonstrated professional growth since your last review?		
3	If you were given suggestions for improvement, document how you worked on them.		
4	What image does your portfolio convey?		
5	Look at your portfolio through the eyes of the reader. What criteria are they looking for?		
6	In addition to presenting accomplishments from the previous review period, present your goals for the next review period.		
7	Show how what you did benefited the organization. Not just "Here is what I did," but "Here is how what I did benefited the company."		
8	Have you met all of the expectations laid out for you? How did you document them?		

9	Make it easy for the reader—at the beginning of the portfolio provide a one-page summary sheet of your accomplishments since the last review.		
10	Did you ask several people to review your portfolio?		
11	Did you evaluate and incorporate their feedback as appropriate?		
12	Have your timelines been realistic?		
13	Are you maintaining your calendar of accountability?		
14			
15			
16			

Section 4. When You Seek to Advance in Your Career

A third benefit of a portfolio applies to those people who want to advance in their careers. In the case of advancement, people are more likely to stay in a field that they are familiar with, and highlighting their experience will play a key role in building this portfolio.

In section 4 we will look at "advancing" from three perspectives: the first example is about moving from one company to another; the second, moving to a job with more responsibility within the same company; and the third, staying in the same position and seeking a higher title. You will notice that many of the hints and tips in one section can be applied to the other two.

Example 1. By Moving to Another Company

The first example highlights the story about a friend of mine who was an event planner for a mid-size pharmaceutical company. She had years of experience and wanted to advance her career by moving to a large multi-national firm. From the examples provided below, you can draw analogies to your field.

- **Research**. As a person with experience in the field, you are expected to have vision and scope—vision to address the many diverse elements that go into the new job, such as marketing, scheduling, and inter-personal relationships... Then you need to thoroughly familiarize yourself with the new company and be able to envision the decision makers who will be involved in your hiring.
- **Gather**. In addition to compiling all your accomplishments you need to include many visuals, especially if you are applying to a people-oriented field.
- **Sequence**. Next, how will you organize the material? For example, one way that the event planner could organize it could be by showcasing her top five to six events, then dividing it into the many divisions with which she had to interface in order to make each event happen. What are some other ways that you could organize this portfolio? Be sure to highlight all the positives that you accomplished—saving money, increasing sales, bringing in new clients—with visuals.
- **Hit the mark**. Finally, we will package the materials in the portfolio to best reflect you. What organizational sequence will you design? Will all accomplishments

have visuals? Will the portfolio be easy for the reader to understand?

Remember the analogy to the trunk filled with examples of your best work experiences? What accomplishments can you showcase to create your best portfolio?

- Thoroughly research the new company and the heads of the departments that could interview you.
- Use the master list that you created when writing your résumé to refresh your memory regarding accomplishments. How do you show your professional growth? Do you go into detail about your most outstanding accomplishments? Try different approaches and see which one makes the most sense to you, represents your values, and will be the most logical to the reader.
- If you have written your functional résumé effectively, your achievements should resonate with the people who will be reading this portfolio (the chief financial officer? the director of marketing? the advertising director? the vice president of sales?). Relate your strengths to each person's department. Have examples that will appeal to each person, showing your accomplishments related that person's division.
- Envision the competition. What makes *you* the perfect candidate for the job?
- Remember—graphics, tables, and charts help. Use your graphic skills to enhance your portfolio.

Your portfolio should answer the key question "Why you?" What makes you stand out from the rest of the candidates applying for the job—some of whom have years of experience and some who are new to the field?

I would like to refer back to a point made in chapter 1 about thank-you letters that relates to this story—pick up on clues learned during the interview. This lesson served my friend very well. During her interview someone commented that she needed to choose between the safe option (staying in her current job) or this new job, which came with a greater upside and more risks. She wasn't sure that she had made her points clear in the interview. So she maximized the value of the thank-you letter.

She wrote a thank-you and let the interviewer know that she had reflected on what he had said and advised him that she wanted the job and acknowledged the risks. She said that her decision would be based on the strength of their offer. In essence she said that she was interested, but she also asked for a strong package to address the risks that the interviewer had raised. Her skills in negotiating developed during her event planning career showed that she could leverage information to her advantage. The thank you demonstrated her interest and that she had the competencies required to be successful at that job.

This short burst of opportunity, the thank-you letter, showed that going the extra mile can make the difference. She got the job.

Checklist #13

By moving to another company

		Status?	Notes to self
1	This portfolio is all about organization and presentation. Its sequencing is determined by you.		
2	Focus on the experience that you will bring to the new position.		
3	In your portfolio, include all departments with which you interacted.		
4	Thoroughly research the new company and the heads of the departments that could interview you.		
5	What is the thread of continuity running through your portfolio? What organizational sequence did you determine?		
6	Envision the different divisions that could send representatives to interview you. Anticipate what each will ask you about.		
7	Highlight achievements that will resonate with each of the divisions with which you might interact.		

8	Envision the competition— some might have years of experience and some might have none. Why should they hire *you*?		
9	What brand—your image—is portrayed in the portfolio?		
10	Did you ask several people to review your portfolio?		
11	Did you evaluate and incorporate their feedback as appropriate?		
12	Have your timelines been realistic?		
13	Are you maintaining your calendar of accountability?		
14			
15			
16			

Example 2. By Moving Up within the Company

Moving up in an organization could require that you change departments. Your advantages could be your accomplishments in your current position, your knowledge of the inner workings of the current and the new area, and the connections and the bridges that you have built within the company. Your advantage is that you are not an unknown factor.

As an example, a project manager advancing within an organization can advance to projects with more responsibility. This could be a new initiative that the company is undertaking such as introducing a new product, managing a company acquired during a merger, or overseeing projects that have greater responsibilities, budgets, and staffing. Here you have to display your energy and enthusiasm as well as your past achievements and your preparedness.

- **Research**. As a person with experience in the company, you are expected to have vision and scope—vision to address the many diverse elements that go into the new job, such as marketing, scheduling, inter-personal relationships… Then you need to thoroughly familiarize yourself with the new project. Do your homework. What does the new job description state? Address each of the key points and show how you would be the best candidate for the position. Are they hiring from within the company or also looking outside?
- **Gather**. In addition to compiling all your accomplishments, you need to have a thread of continuity that demonstrates how your accomplishments in your current job have prepared you for the new position.
- **Sequence**. Next, how will you organize the material? Similar to the event planner, one way would be to showcase several big projects that you oversaw, then relate the responsibilities from your current job to the new position. Be sure to highlight all the common benefits such as your overall knowledge of the company, the bridges that you have built, and your positive reputation within the company.
- **Hit the mark**. Finally, we will package the materials in the portfolio to best reflect you. What organizational sequence will you design? Will all accomplishments have visuals? Will the portfolio be easy for the reader to understand?
- What examples would best demonstrate your management style? What examples would you provide to show

that you are able to take on greater responsibilities? Handle a larger budget? Manage a larger staff? Delegate more broadly?

- If the position that you are applying for has much greater responsibility, show why you are the best candidate for the job. Your examples should be evidence based. Use visuals extensively—charts, tables, and other graphics.

By moving up within the company

		Status?	Notes to self
1	If moving up requires you to change departments, demonstrate how you have built bridges within the organization.		
2	If the position you are interviewing for has much greater responsibility, show why you are the best candidate for the job.		
3	Use graphics, charts, and other visuals to show how your accomplishments relate to the new position.		
4	Do not use "I've been here a long time" as your justification for a promotion.		
5	What image does your portfolio convey? Does it look like you spent a lot of time on it?		
6	Did you ask several people with excellent editing skills to review your portfolio?		
7	Did you evaluate and incorporate their feedback as appropriate?		
8	Have your timelines been realistic?		
9	Are you maintaining your calendar of accountability?		

10			
11			
12			

Example 3. By Seeking a New Job Title

The previous examples have focused on jobs in the private sector. The public sector is different. Jobs in the public sector at the federal, state, or local level often have published criteria that candidates are expected to meet in order to be promoted or be retained.

This example focuses on someone who wanted a higher job title in her department at a university. I will let you in on the secret to success. Having worked at several large public universities, I was surrounded by people who had master's and doctoral degrees and who had outstanding accomplishments. Yet some could not get promoted. Finally, they would come to me, and I would review their portfolio. It would be all over the place. The job they were going for had certain criteria, but they did not address them. They never specifically cited how they met the criteria, in order to warrant the promotion, tenure, or being rehired. The school wanted them to demonstrate A, B, and C, and they were off on a creative writing streak. No. Give the readers what they want.

For this type of portfolio, we will switch the order: research, sequence, gather, and hit the mark. The sequence has already been determined—by the template of the job criteria. It is your job to stick to that sequence and gather your accomplishments to showcase them in the required order.

- Many people think that a job with published criteria is one of the easiest types of portfolios to write because the outline—the template—is already given to you. They are right. Just follow the outline! It is there for a reason.

- Keep your accomplishments in the same sequence as the printed criteria. Use the printed criteria as your template.
- As in the case of all portfolios, your accomplishments have already happened. There is no new writing. Just present your achievements in the required sequence.
- Make sure that you are working from the most recent list of criteria. If you last applied several years ago, the criteria might have been updated. Working from old criteria will not make the best impression on the reader.
- Find out the rating system. Particularly focus on those criteria that have a higher points value.
- Read the criteria thoroughly and gather all relevant material. Time after time applicants would submit "the same old same old." This year's portfolio would look just like last year's. There would be no evidence of forward movement, no evidence of any type of professional growth or leadership.
- Back up each of your claims with documentation. For example, if you spoke at a conference, scan the cover page and the page showing your topic, and include it in the portfolio.
- Follow the rules. Research the time regulations. For example, if the policy says that you have to wait a minimum of two years between promotions, wait the appropriate time. Someone has been assigned the job of checking the dates.
- Unfortunately, we are living in a litigious society. You should document every claim that you make.

- "I've been here a long time" is *not* a justification for a promotion. Present evidence of meeting the criteria in the template.
- What image does your portfolio convey? Does it look like you spent a lot of time on it or that you decided to submit it at the last minute? Readers can tell the difference.

If your organization has a template and it is unwieldy, make the template work for you. Here is an example of what my friend did. She was an Associate Professor teaching student therapists in the Physical Therapy Department and was applying to be promoted to Professor, and one of the main criteria was that she had to demonstrate was leadership, which she had. However, there was no category in any of the three criteria—teaching, scholarship, or service—labeled for "leadership." Teaching would be the most logical place to show academic leadership.

Visually compare appendix F, which is the university's not-user-friendly template, to appendix G, the same material in an easy-to-edit and easy-to-understand template:

Column1	Column 2	Column 3
The criteria, with the text from the template copied directly below it	The standard, with the text from the template copied directly below it	Documentation, where you provide material to prove that you did something that met the criteria and the standard

The document proving your claim goes right below the box. This way there can be *no* question about whether the applicant met the criteria. For mastery of the subject, she included a scanned version of her teaching observation by a well-respected professional in the field of physical therapy and a certificate that showed that she was a program reviewer. Even though an observation was not required at her level, my friend wanted to show that she was always willing to improve.

In appendix G, "Teaching," my friend addressed all four sections of criteria 1, "Teaching," and *added* a fifth section, "Program Administration." You cannot rewrite the agreed-upon criteria; however, you can take the agreed-upon criteria and make the format work for you. Her goal was to show the readers—which could include people from outside her area—that she had indeed taken on leadership responsibilities.

Checklist #15

By seeking a new job title

		Status?	Notes to self
1	In the public sector, there is usually a list of job criteria. That makes this one of the easiest portfolios to write. The template has already been written for you. Just follow it.		
2	Ensure that you are working from the most recent list of criteria.		
3	Find out the rating system. Particularly focus on those criteria that have a higher points value.		
4	Follow all timelines.		
5	Do not just resubmit the same old portfolio. Show professional growth and leadership.		
6	Make the template your own.		
7	Use graphics, charts, and other visuals to highlight your accomplishments.		
8	Is each accomplishment clearly labeled?		
9	Include all licenses and certification.		
10	Do not use "I've been here a long time" as your justification for a promotion.		

11	What image does your portfolio convey? Does it look like you spent a lot of time on it or that you decided to submit it at the last minute?		
12	Did you ask several people with excellent editing skills to review your portfolio?		
13	Did you evaluate and incorporate their feedback as appropriate?		
14	Have your timelines been realistic?		
15	Are you maintaining your calendar of accountability?		
16			
17			
18			

Section 5. Package Yourself Professionally

When presenting a portfolio, it's easy to weigh it down with too many examples. It is completely understandable to want to present as much work as possible, especially if you are proud of your accomplishments. However, try stepping into the reader's shoes. An extremely large portfolio can be overwhelming, causing the reader to possibly not read it thoroughly. Each entry should be significant, not repetitive.

How is a portfolio packaged? A portfolio can be a digital website or a paper-based binder. Think about the image that you want to convey with your portfolio. Before the digital age, people would have a three-ring binder that they brought with them to the interview, to showcase their work. You could still do that; however...

Today's business runs at a fast pace.

- Will the reader actually sit there and read through a three-ring binder in a thorough way? Probably not.
- Also, with a three-ring binder you are walking in "cold." A digital portfolio can be sent in advance of a meeting.
- A digital portfolio will save you the time and expense of photocopying a binder and reconfiguring the material for each interview.
- Finally, unless you make a duplicate copy of the binder, you will need to take the binder with you at the end of the meeting, so there is no "leave-behind" that the interviewer can refer back to.

Some people assume that the work they are presenting is more important than how it is presented. Not true. The technology holding your work, whether it is a website or a binder, is as important as the content. Make the portfolio look outstanding, because everything you do goes toward creating your brand.

- One major advantage of having a website is that a website is not linear like a book or a binder. Therefore, it is a time-saver that allows you to easily customize your material for each interview that you go on. For example, in your cover letter, you might highlight jobs A, B, C, D, and E. However, for another position, you might prioritize jobs E, A, D, C, and then B. You do not have to do any rearrangement. With a website, all the reader has to do is click on the link for job A or job C on your home page. There is no sequencing or prioritizing.

Web Design

Our motto is "If an eight-year-old can design a website, so can I."

Perhaps you are a web design expert. Great. Skip this section. For the rest of us, let's get started.

- When you send your materials to a prospective employer, it makes you look contemporary to have a digital portfolio.
- Gone are the days when you had to know HTML code to create a website. If you can type on a computer and save the text, you can create a basic website.
- If you have ever added an attachment to an email, you can upload your saved files to your website. The concept is the same.
- More importantly, a website is an efficient way to keep everything that you want an interviewer to read in one easy-to-access place, rather than sending a lot of email attachments. A decision maker is not going to sit there opening an email attachment, then another email attachment, then....
- Keep your website simple and easy to navigate. You are not creating a website for a multinational corporation.
- Do not make your website part of an existing website, such as a personal website. No reader wants to wade through one site to get to another.
- *PC Magazine* is a reliable source for technology information and there are a lot of free, easy-to-use sources *(https://www.pcmag.com/picks/the-best-website-builders)*. Try a few sites listed, and see which one you feel is the easiest for you to use.

The advantage of the digital portfolio version is that you can cite the URL in your résumé and your cover letter, and a portfolio can be an effective selling tool before you meet with the interviewer.

The rules for a paper-based binder and a digital portfolio are basically the same:

- Convey a professional image.
- Include your résumé, certificates and licenses, and samples of your achievements.
- Include any documents that praise the outcome of an initiative—for example, an email from a supervisor stating that an initiative you created brought in one hundred new customers last week, a major project that was completed on time, or a cost saver or a revenue enhancer.
- Present examples that show your professionalism and resourcefulness. Demonstrate what makes you the best candidate for this job.
- Clearly label each document so that the reader instantly knows what they are looking at.
- Be consistent. Refer to a document by the same name in your résumé, your cover letter, and your portfolio.
- Consider ease of use.

Here are some points that will help you make your portfolio user-friendly:

- There should be a thread of continuity running through your résumé, your cover letter, and your portfolio regarding the names you give to documents.
- Create clear filenames so that people looking at your portfolio know what they are looking at.
- Bring in a fresh set of unbiased eyes.

- Family and friends might give you new insights about selecting your best works.
- Do they think that you presented the material in a logical order?
- Do they think that you focused on your accomplishments?
- Basically, do they understand the points you were trying to make?
- Ask them to describe the image that your portfolio presented.

In conclusion, if there are criteria by which candidates are being rated, you want to be rated against the highest criteria. Don't be better than the worst. Be the best! Have your portfolio be the icing on the cake. Remember—the job hunt is not the place for subtlety.

Checklist #16

Package yourself professionally

		Status?	Notes to self
1	The packaging is just as important as the content. What image do you want to convey in your portfolio? Are you hitting the mark?		
2	Each accomplishment should be significant, not redundant.		
3	There should be a thread of continuity running through your portfolio. Going from section to section should not be jarring.		
4	Make sure that all documents are clearly labeled.		
5	Include document that praise your work performance.		
6	Present examples of your professionalism and resourcefulness. Demonstrate why you are the best candidate for this job.		
7	Be consistent in the naming of your accomplishments.		
8	Ensure that the portfolio is user friendly and easy to navigate.		
8	Did you ask several people to review your portfolio?		

9	Do not send your material as an email with attachments.		
10	Have your timelines been realistic?		
11	Are you maintaining your calendar of accountability?		
12			
13			
14			

Wrapping It Up

For you this is definitely not the end; it is just the beginning. It's exciting. Yes, a new job makes us all nervous and excited. It's the start of something "new," and we all need some adventure in our lives. Hopefully, you will go back and re-read sections on an "as-needed" basis.

What were the major points that I was trying to make? The first is that there is no one "right" way to do this. We went from the general to the specific meaning that many job search elements are the same—the résumé, the cover letter, the thank-you letter. How we branch off and personalize them is what makes the process unique. We look for different jobs. Our creativity causes us to create different portfolios. Yet we all come back again toward a common goal— getting the job.

Hopefully, you have done some introspection. You know what stage of your career you are in. You have been able to acknowledge your accomplishments and present them to others in an interesting way to others.

What are your ten greatest achievements?

Does your résumé sparkle?

Is all of your correspondence error free?

When we look back on our journey, do you feel that you have reinvented yourself? Reinvigorated yourself? Are you happy with the image that you portray to the interviewer? Is your résumé working for you? Are you building on the interview relationship with your thank-you emails? Are you happy with your portfolio?

We are part of a process that people have followed for hundreds of years and will continue to follow for hundreds more. Naturally, the jobs have changed; the technology has evolved. Yet almost every job hunter over the centuries has gone through the same process.

One of the best quotes I ever heard is "No is just the answer to a different question." Someone will say, "Yes, welcome to our company."

I wish you the best of luck!

Appendix A

Sample Action Words for a Functional Résumé

Below are just a few action words that can give the decision maker an overview of your capabilities. As you look at samples of functional résumés you will find many more.

Analyzed	Evaluated
Applied	Increased
Assembled	Maintained
Communicated	Managed
Constructed	Organized
Created	Planned
Demonstrated	Redesigned
Designed	Scheduled
Engaged	Set up
Established	Solved

There are many helpful websites, such Indeed, that can help you find action words to suit your career and experience.

Chronological Résumé

Like all résumés, chronological résumés contain your contact information, a summary statement, work experience, and education. Unlike the functional résumé, the experience section of the chronological résumé will detail your work history and experience in each role, with job title and dates, beginning with most recent job.

- **Header**. Include your name, email address, and phone number.

- **Summary/objective**. This is the objective related to position being applied for. Core qualifications can be included.

- **Professional experience**. This is your employment history. List your most recent company with job title and dates in that position. Detail experience and accomplishments in each position.

- **Education**: Put your highest-level degree first. List degree and school.

Appendix C

Functional Résumé

Functional résumés and chronological résumés contain similar information but are organized differently. Functional résumés highlight a person's skills and accomplishments without aligning to specific jobs or time periods. This is especially useful if you have gaps in employment or are switching industries. An employment history may be included by way of listing positions and companies toward the end, without including dates.

- **Header**. Include your name, email address, and phone number.

- **Summary/objective**. This is the objective related to the position being applied for. Core qualifications can be included.

- **Experiences and skills**. List your accomplishments.

- **Employment history**. List your most recent company and job title. You may exclude dates. Be prepared to detail the timeline in an interview.

- **Education**. Put your highest-level degree first. List degree and school.

Outline for the Cover Letter

Dear _____:

Attached is my résumé for the position of _____.

Paragraph 1: explain why you want this job.

Paragraph 2: give two to three short reasons why you are qualified for this job.

Paragraph 3: give two to three short reasons why you would excel at this job.

Paragraph 4: give two to three short examples of how you will contribute to the organization.

Paragraph 5: include a polite closing, and if you have a digital portfolio, include the URL here.

Sincerely,

(use a script font if possible)

Appendix E

Outline for the Thank-You Letter

Dear _____:

Thank you for the opportunity to interview with you on April 26 for the position of _____.

Paragraph 1: from points raised during the interview, recap why you are qualified for this job.

Paragraph 2: from points raised during the interview, recap why you would excel at this job.

Paragraph 3: from points raised during the interview, recap how you know that you will contribute to the organization.

Paragraph 4: include a polite closing.

Sincerely,

(use a script font if possible)

Appendix F

Promotion Criteria

Criteria 1. Teaching

Mastery of subject

Criteria	Standards
Subject mastery	Strong peer observations (above average to excellent) Leadership in local, national, and international organizations
Student engagement	Positive feedback from students, internship supervisors, and employers
Course development, assessment, and redesign to incorporate student use of technology across the curriculum	Ongoing development, updating, and redesign of courses integrated with and supportive of technology standards
Professional development	Ongoing participation in courses, conferences, and workshops in one's discipline Collaboration with colleagues both within the university and also in the greater online learning community

Appendix G

Promotion Criteria Rearranged

For Criteria 1, Teaching

Criteria 1, Teaching, consists of the following:

- Section 1, Subject Mastery
- Section 2, Student Engagement
- Section 3, Course Development, Assessment, and Redesign
- Section 4, Professional Development
- Section 5, Program Administration

Section 1. Subject mastery

Criteria	Standard	Documents
Subject mastery	Strong peer evaluation	Observation by Dr. John Smith, Director of the Physical Therapy Department, Mountainside Hospital
	Leadership in local, national, and international organizations	"Currently, I am active in two organizations: • the International Physical Therapy Educators' Society, where I serve as a program reviewer for graduate physical therapy programs • the Association of Physical Therapy Educators, where I serve as Editor of the *Journal of Physical Therapy Educators*"

Strong Peer Evaluation

Below you will find an observation conducted by Dr. John Smith, Director of the Physical Therapy Department at Mountainside Hospital. I invited Dr. Smith, a knowledge expert in the field of physical therapy education, to provide his professional feedback regarding the course Emerging Issues in Physical Therapy, which I teach online in the summer I semester.

Section 5. Program administration

Criteria	Standard	Documents
Program administration	Proven academic leadership	"In addition to recertification and administration of the Master's Degree in Physical Therapy, I have been working on policies and procedures to make access to and progress through the university a user-friendly process for the students."
	Areas of responsibility	"Currently, my areas of responsibility include: • Chairing the Master's Degree in Physical Therapy • Overseeing the creation of the new Doctorate in Physical Therapy"